Cliffhanger Notes

Cliffhanger Notes

Dennis Lucas

Left Hand Books

The publisher gratefully acknowledges the John W. and Clara C. Higgins Foundation for its generous support in the funding of this book.

Designed by Bryan McHugh.

Distributed by SPD, Berkeley, CA.
Left Hand Books website: lefthandbooks.com

ISBN 1-880516-30-6

Manufactured in the United States of America.

CONTENTS

Postcards from Outer Space

All art is quite useless.
—Oscar Wilde, *The Picture of Dorian Gray*

broken tongues whispering stories through cold empty hands wearing a white baseball glove on a withered stump / flowers falling from the ceiling in a half-conscious dream / a rose on the white coffin

badly burned by the good years / nonsense puddles in the hall / tear up the little scraps of paper put an end to all this waiting / bored into submission like a hot water potato chip gun or canceled stamp eyes burning away in the moonlight

breaking glass on a haunted porch / kicking emotions around the tomb wearing delicate ballet hiking cleats

given the hook instead of a parade

void the line reserved for understanding

twenty more years of dull ghosts in the forecast / sustained by a baboon liver they found lurking in the dirt behind the trailer

flowers drowning in sunlight

no need to enroll in more idiot lessons / no pony rides back to the womb

singing along with TV commercials like a lobotomized former Miss America

mop up the blinding darkness with a dying man's tarot card
fiery edges of death glimmering in his eyes like flaming bowl-
ing balls / cut it loose sever the ties let the wind take it intro-
duce it to dust / your breathing is not precious

black ice / a bullet-riddled child / terminal misspelling / the
ghost of a bathtub

a love song on the radio blackened both of his eyes

twenty to life without being formally charged with anything
jail made him memorize every line of Carl Sandburg

dreams so strange they were made to stay in the guest room
/ watches went dead whenever you entered / he painted a
picture of the noose before he used it

dreams not included

find a purpose a place to fit in and hide any reason to endure
will do / inch after inch the train gets there / throw away the
pieces of paper

this is a necessary waste of time and energy

palace gates melting like wax to alert the masses that all bets
were off no cockfights on a day when even the village idiot
had the sense to stay inside and stare at the walls or risk sum-
mary execution in front of his entire bloodline

catch it like a dead animal and run / there is no point give up / be afraid of the dark

hands tied with pieces of sky / ghost drips haunt the sink

points of interest to the left everything else to the right / blank parts blank pages / waiting around takes a lifetime / reduce it all to ash / polish the crown of nightmares / tears streaming down the face of a wax dummy

yield succumb submit

the crow turns into a dog and barks at the shadow of the river / reading dirty windows like a book / a long ride nowhere in the car / that was easy / who ever said that pain hurt / silence repossessed us / no room for another image only lucid whims / yellow nicotine-stained fingers

just might get there in the time it takes to live

she was sitting on the phone trying to hatch it into a green thumb / anything can happen but won't / paint peeling dust falling like rain / letter after letter unanswered / flexed monkey muscle on the side of a coffee cup / hold the pen properly / the task at hand blinded him

burn all bridges before crossing them

contagious noise / painful glances

bottled inches of wind listening to time pass with glass ears /
it has been the same year for a decade now

an ashtray suckling a fish / evil clowns handing out internal
suntans to the children

cutting the tongue out of a dead man's mouth / scramble
the messages / former altar boys committing atrocities with
a fly swatter / the sun throws its garbage in the street / torn
clocks / glass of life spilled on a shivering corpse fed through
a shredder

jet chalk lining the sky / moss sideburns

one-legged ghosts limping up and down the corridor of the
mind / wrong script / black Band-aid / wooden hair

sniffing gasoline in the shed conjuring angels demons and
aliens / burning books in the woods horrible writing from an
old notebook burned in a campfire last day of school

never apologize unless you are sorry

cryptic birthday cake on a picnic table / forgotten conversation

claw the eye that sees you puncture the lungs that breathe
you

coal mined from a receding hairline / tired voice on a dead

phone / cops chasing kids from a haunted house / follow a
chore to the grave / play the game and lose like everyone else

a bad mood for a gift / stolen cigars in the socks

a painted face on a broken mirror / they saw his heels swing-
ing in the attic window / insanity like a bony finger pointing
at X-rays of clouds

the suspense isn't killing me

she loves him even after he tried to shoot her four times
even after he tried to kill her with the hatchet she bought
him for Valentine's Day

mice grew the food and bartered it for chemical winks / slam-
ming doors on mental fingers / emptiness all over again /
endless can opener crowbar hauntings

celluloid curl of hair

put away the flowers and get out the bullets

bird nests in her eyes with fat men sitting in them / street
lamps blinking off to steal from parked cars

have no claim to fame / trade in your war stories for psychic
envelopes mailed to the enemy / chew these words slowly let
them break your teeth / it all must go paper clearance

forgetting remembering stopping beginning

I've seen cowboys die on TV and have learned nothing from it

wanting in on the way out

an invisible lottery

robbing a cerebral head-candy bank

just get on with something / add nothing was the first ingredient of the recipe / sick unhealthy life / angry puppets faking seizures like wet rugs tossed from the back of a rainbow

disease is getting the best of us

ghosts constantly remind us of all that is missing

white silence counterfeiting words / tin brainwash / haunted bodies stringing dawn like an instrument / invisible keys rusty intangible locks

clothe the dead in bright darkness free their eyes like birds

a kite fell from the sky crippling the neighbors' children as if they were twigs under foot / white swings feet touching green branches under blue sky / a recess of pink cars

a pissed-in genie bottle

when they come will you be adequately armed

yes yes yes silence no no no more silence

the Elvis Christ was sighted walking on eggshells

glimpses at the lack of magic / envelopes filled with smoke /
lapping time from the palm of an idiot / rainy crossroads teeth
/ canceled parade lobotomy / trees coughing in unison / dust
that never settles / electric can-opener moonshine / elusive
truths buried in the hills / ice cream melting in a coffin / an
ant dragging off summer / cross the days off the calendar
before they happen this way nothing will surprise you

the clock is a little fast I'm a little slow

the future is a blind dog

be your own eccentric old lady

thimble smiles bucket frowns

there is no light no tunnel / open the sky like a piñata / or-
ange flame from a pink lighter touched to bright red lipstick

producing golden carbon at the liquid margins of the lip-sculpted end / the birds were flying off with the flowers to decorate their nests the gardener was considering buying a gun he could only take so much before the training wheels fell off his dump truck / selling the hot dog truck to strangers was the worst thing that ever happened to them / grandpa had a false premonition

he walked into the party two weeks dead with the noose still around his neck / nothing to say / now I lay me down to sleep jaded tired on the verge of little / crawling toward emerald cigarettes

a corkscrew tearing into a melon

one of the cows had been sneaking out at night into the neighbor's barn and dialing 1-900 numbers until dawn

dead negatives torn pictures from childhood

there is no place like not home

a canvas as large as a house stretched over a field of milk / a dead catfish floating by

his sister came in to show him her new tattoo but he wasn't interested so she went down to the basement and shot herself a suicide note was left on the refrigerator door but disappeared unread old women carrying gravity in plastic bags hunching over they stare at the sidewalk

detectives out the window trying not to act like detectives / empty frames film melts on the projector bulb the audience moans and voices its discontent

fall as far as possible / dead cold foreign lips / a single brain cell

grandma liked pornography her motto was don't fuck it up for everyone else

spending time like coins / a crow eating itself like an old tire / deathbed parade / gray sidewalk / never enter Army recruiter buildings / gray stubble on the face of the corpse

you don't know me he screamed at his parents you're right they said

a recurring feeling of hopelessness

abstract noses blown in the womb / straws in the cogs of the wheels of power

no one stopped a clock for a second few even bothered to try / he beat the clock so he wore gloves to avoid injury

clumsy trees line dancing on the Nashville Network

stopwatch grass growing at ringside

feather coffins

compromising invisible attitudes

born blank each morning

boundless inches of paranoid miles under the belt

they are fooling you with their success / a rusty trophy / skel-
etons absorbing bad energy / empty mirror empty stomach
beer and cigarettes

nonlinear hellos at ground zero

the seed that grew you turns into a darkened cemetery plot
with the hides of deer in it shadows of children without child-
hoods turned the blue pools of your eyes into fire hydrants
pissed on by dogs / bleeding crying out for help into a sev-
ered phone

it's a shame she had to grow up there were so many excuses
for her as a child

he sued himself and won blew the top of his head off with a
defective toaster oven then poured himself a drink / man of
leisure with bed sheet skin

a spider walking across the flaming edge of a lemon in an airtight frame / the window swallows my vision and spits it out over rooftops and streets marred with potholes

an outlet whispering the secrets of the ages / new Jell-O furniture

fiddle while Rome burns / sky written simultaneously world-wide so it could be read anywhere on Earth / an empty stare

end send spend lend

sun rising above the mountain / golden baby carriages pushed by chickens / it wasn't Eden not then not now

the cat yawns like a lampshade / the plot thins

bury a prized possession in the yard

Jesus lost his eyes in a factory accident

take the couch to the vet for its shots / lock the evil TV in its room / build a cardboard coffin to float home in / read ten books at once / you can't yes you can another another an-other / watered down bad art / a phantom knocks on the window to wave hello / mind beaten into the dirt / Kennedy's face on all the matchbooks drinking champagne and eating codeine with a virtual stranger at sunrise

walked around Manhattan for three hours four people spoke to me can you spare any change sir excuse me sir I'm starving can you spare any change smoke coke hash dude how was your day guy

postcards from outer space

this concludes this evening's broadcast

limits know no limits

the hum of a fan on a forgotten afternoon

the page is getting smaller / enough of this cruel joke

rated X stamped on the side of a glassine bag / in no condition period / burn it all or rebuild it

in love with what doesn't matter / how much more can we take before we break down anyway / none of this is good enough disregard everything you have learned

pornographic sun

seizure the day / return to the loam

fractions of people

bless me for I am unholy then again don't I'm a fucking saint

going nowhere fast with scarecrow agility

kites tied to dead animals along the highway / freshly mowed grass changing into butterflies white smoke-stained curtains / think I'll cut myself off after this last sip of gasoline he said

peeled from the couch like an orange / the moon shaving its legs

nothing but the sound of rain repeating itself on the windows of a cold apartment

gold stopwatch control group net for minnow-dipping / questions any realizations yet / pink balloons plugged into a cornfield

the TV bleeds / this is not a fair fight / trophies melted for bullets snap of a bb hitting the mayor's eye

so long forever

wigs for bowling balls

she had a hair spray fracture and couldn't come to the phone an infant went into labor in the sandbox during recess the principal called the National Guard but they weren't home he left a message on their machine but they never got back to him another child eight years old brought one of the original copies of the Declaration of Independence for show-and-tell proceeded to light it on fire while rubbing herself with a fly swatter

contraceptive TV cigarettes / refracted rainbow salad / tombstone shoelace picnic basket

burn the little scraps of paper

sound of birds falling in the window

application for sainthood denied again

arthritic fingers of trees poking the open air in the eyes

what to say into a silent phone

in-laws and outlaws in the same church pew

puddle on roof reflecting the fire escape pigeons evaporating in a dog eye like playground soap

a bloated gun broken globe white sink pink snow rusty tambourine icy cold memory of sunlight on a carpet / sneaky halo menacing a rubber toothpick / childhood escapes out a crack in the window

what would you order if you went to dinner with Jesus

a tree fell in the yard sounding like thousands of cartoon bricks being instantly thrown together to make a wall / sirens chirp down a sidestreet like angry metallic birds / pick any moment steal another memory

wind in the heart a cardiac breeze under skin

yellow Walkman red lawn mower green grass blue sky

hide in your room for at least a decade

frost on the playpen

bad evil rotten notebook / have no more to do with it

sitting in someone else's room for a living / a reproduction of a reproduction Van Gogh portrait in a cheap frame

if it's true it's also false

drunkenly cutting off locks of hair at random burning them in the ashtray / if you will die for me I'll will you five dollars spider webs holding heads together

let the characters in unwritten stories die carry them to the fireplace

only in America or somewhere else

conversations dwindle like pissed-on campfires / a barbwire parachute traded for a crab meat chandelier / enjoy it now while you can

math homework scribbled on the soles of his feet

put the past to sleep / unplug the TV / fall on your face / tail between the legs

volcanic runway

gray cat has a junk habit sneaks out at night shooting dope with all the money it steals by day / old songs gone up in green smoke like blind men betting money

marble egg shattered on the sidewalk / dead apple tree in moonlight / pink milk / dusty blinds / harpsichord music / freeze this moment don't try to decipher it let all these scraps of paper and fragments of broken writing remain static / let's let go

when we left off our hero was waiting for an excuse a reason to endure / his leading lady was a professional widower with the cure for nothing

we leave our hero clinging to a thread of possibility for now

is the Good Book good enough

this is getting us nowhere where could it possibly lead / a sudden burst of bland energy what to do with it pacing the room sitting in a chair / monkeys screeching in their cages like electric can openers / everything is under control don't worry but panic immediately

a town where all the clocks are broken

he saw more than one of himself in the mirror

a scar shaped like a fortune cookie on her arm she ran her fingers over it and felt a piece of paper which she pulled out and read don't believe in anything

karate smoke rings

the house absorbed his worst tendencies and had him evicted

a pocket chain saw / shrapnel in the shadow

lost toys escaping the flames that claimed the insane asylum your uncle went up in

alibi hairpin tango fire-eating organ-donor candy oil

he hated poems but wrote them all the time

death is everywhere it gets on your clothes never comes out /
under intellectual scrutiny things appeared evil and illusory

never venture past the obvious / one life not to live

a pig wearing a tuxedo at daybreak

some people really believe Elvis is still alive

elderly tenants in slow motion jumping out their windows to
the street

he took off his mask and threw it across the room like a horse-
shoe

doing the right thing meant staying in bed / the mental radio
only played static

here gone absent

cheap lamps pointed at ceilings

dragged along like a dog without legs

morning was carried away by twenty empty wheelbarrows /
an alarm clock in a morgue / wilted light bulb flowers limp-
ing toward a rain shelter / lost on an infinite map

bar with electric chairs instead of stools / cobwebs on the
jukebox / a spastic insult from an anorexic mind / the wind
must be out drinking or praying

pollinated tombstones / pouring tea in little china cups for
dolls without faces

the landlord of my logic constantly changes the locks and
calls in death threats

a flag over a day camp for onions / wallpaper pregnancies or
clay cartwheels inspiring a pasta guillotine / wearing piñata
hard hats / rainbow flesh / amphetamine toast / an intrave-
nous grilled cheese sandwich

a child's crude drawing of heaven nailed to the smile of a
clown / lips like lynched earthworms / an insect shoveling
dirt on a telephone book

the doctor entered the operating room wearing a dirty sock
over his mouth

envelope-flavored gum like a soggy tombstone / canteen filled with thumbtacks like a violin playing the entrails of a duck

let the cat out

not this again / get to the next page before an angel reads over your shoulder and ruins it

don't learn anything that might distract you from yourself

in Macys they saw Andy Warhol browsing the aisles she walked up to him and said I don't really like your work but I felt like I had to say hello to you oh that's ok I make a new friend everyday

I'll never win by these rules / I was a fool and luckily still am / pay no attention to this

onion skin paper in the wood stove

alligator shoelaces crow hat placebo sponge toothpaste meat

there is no pulse

blazing a trail through the woods to the moon / long road nowhere under embryonic light bulbs / crime-riddled baldness / it might be fine later

blank straw ghost prom king

when I don't paint my masterpiece I want you to not be there
/ goat bee coffin bathtub Hula-Hoop soup bone volcanic harp
residue rainbow smokestack / sixty-first second of a minute /
even incoherence lapses into incoherence

he got his shadow pierced at the mall by some guy who didn't
know what the hell he was doing

a car alarm goes off in the street like a programmed rooster
with mile-long feathers

drive toward what will happen divorce it cut it away like can-
cer or instant fossils / ignore the grail / the sound of ice in a
mirror / an inchworm measuring itself with a golden ruler

purple coffee cup green breath mints / imagination stepped
like a huge foot into a room of hands / Trojan Horse filled
with hollow logic / the museum-rapers fucked all the paint-
ings and left bloody condoms everywhere

do this do that don't do this don't do that you know the drill
/ between here there and nowhere / standing while seated in
a chair / hair flowing out of a bald head / the could-have-
beens added up to what actually happened

drown the lifeguard beat the boxer paint the painter

take this barren gift as a religious offering of sorts / marble
Indian newspapers soaking up an oil spill / a rose by any other

name still smells like smoke

death to the old notebooks

writing with invisible ink on a lampshade

you will be first to say hello I will stare vacantly at you / let someone else deal with it / Americans don't want literature they want Spielberg comic books / miracle fungus tonic wayward crop-duster

enter the slug salon

you wouldn't understand

Christmas kisses with lit cigarettes in mouth / insulted infant art / impatient library books / orgasm mailed C.O.D. to other planets / this is mine don't touch it

none of this is helping

he had an intense fear of animals reading his discarded mail so he tore it up like confetti / he stood on a chair for hours on end as if posing for a portrait just so he could complain about how tired his legs were

an epileptic parabola / an ice cube in hot sun desperately feeling around for a pen to write an impromptu will he bit into a clock to try and taste time all it did for him was break a tooth time flies anyway fun or not / a bird stole his memory used it for part of its nest / rubber baby in plastic carriage

he moved to the next town which was two inches away / tattoos on headless puppets from New Jersey / Live Free or Die My Ass / three crows like bad guys in a Western on the verge of flying off somewhere / we never understood him but we were cheap and petty we didn't have a chance and didn't know the difference / mindless imps little hands feeding their little heads

hail disasters

filthy rich sundial salesman wearing a meat locker tiara / black tire yellow rope tied to a limb

go to hell for the company heaven for the temperature

an American sees someone drive by in a Cadillac and thinks I want that Cadillac a Frenchman sees the same and thinks someday he'll walk like me / this space has been reserved / he had to find a new illusion / rubber ax bouncing off cement wood / blood-stained blueprints / no substance / glimpses at dead air frozen pieces of never

learning how to play the gun as a musical instrument

he smoked his ballet program / alligator mouth shut with a refrigerator hum / blinding sunlight / Neanderthal etchings / weather for sale over the telephone / metal cricket outside

you don't look so good his tenant said to the grand piano that had never been played his tenant always talked to the piano instead of speaking to him directly

the ship surfaces every ten years so local ghosts can rob its treasure

operators are standing by

milk cow squeeze lemon strike match

too much light makes the dark show / I leave you with this and this as well

rubber-heeled tree stump

he was a pseudo-intellectual who wasn't sure if something was better than nothing

the bathtub was used as his coffin / the bookshelf served as his wallet / rusty silverware / a lame rubber duck in a time capsule / too lazy to rewrite / he was so poor he couldn't even pay attention

the final moment really did come one day

his bald spot took up an entire room

kill the king burn the churches libraries museums

wet crows touching down on bare branches for a split second / whittle the pages down / stranger behind the mask behind the mask

he could afford to take great risks / his diamond hernia was acting up and down the main stage / I cannot will not endure your comments / free at last never came / a runaway band of silver balloons over Brooklyn / I told him that I'd just had a lobotomy and I was relearning everything / they say true disciples are always repulsive / it seemed suspicious to see a library open at night

tattered smiles shooting buckshot at phantoms / praying to small things / the children traded their favorite baseball cards for fish heads / plastic motorcycle tents inhaling green lawns / stand up turn to dust / cows eating grass growing from an abandoned couch beside a stream / one-rung ladder for a soul / this is not a test / cotton candy hand attachments on all the children

studying Turkish by candlelight

they took a long walk together and when they returned they no longer knew who they were some stay in a subway car for their entire lives for lack of anything better to do

Euripides vs. Captain Marvel

junk mail delivered by dead monkeys on a Sunday / depressing tenements slithering subway cars

he got so drunk on the night of his retirement dinner that he forgot that he had ever worked a day in his life / forever grinning at the void no desire to do anything like a small door opening into a catastrophe that never made the local papers

three brown shattered bird eggs blown from a nest shadows without bodies never will be missed or mourned never fly never catch a worm never make a nest for their young disappearing forever without the world having blinked even once

the talentless the mediocre and insane always sought him out

by the time his brother finally fell down dead his blood had nearly covered the entire playground

a millionaire's finger probing a pay phone's coin return slot

always break the promises you make to yourself

they exchanged social security numbers at a flea market

the phone only rang on Tuesdays no one knew why

he could never complete a thought so he was always frustrated

she had taken to spending her holidays in the attic the last
few years trying on old wigs in dusty sunlight humming old
songs to herself holding old dresses in front of herself in a
broken mirror like a laundromat plugged into a hanging

baring his teeth blessing himself in the doorway / dust in the
holy water / a gift-wrapped profile in the mirror / stone pulse
of corpses like a river running into a vacuum cleaner or house
made of old clothing / his tongue rolled up like an old rug

heavily armed in the living room / birds by the dozen hang-
ing from little ropes in the branches

a truck ran over her hair

I can see the string holding the clouds above the buildings /
the citadel / sun shining through the dirt / beds soaked with
gasoline / wilted flowers rusty doorbells in legal-size enve-
lopes / another feather in his plastic dunce cap / it is finally
coming together

she tries to feed the pigeons but they can tell she is sick so
they won't go near her / they had nothing to say to each other
and became great friends / the car in his head had stalled
and run out of gas / obscene phone calls made by nature

during a drought / he only wanted what he could carry in a bowling bag

coins baked in bread / standard cardboard raindrops like crows talking to each other on the sidewalk after work / people look so silly and precious when carrying umbrellas

I saw a bird look both ways and run across the street / a dog tied outside a supermarket its master is inside shopping the endless aisles of my tired skull

only one ship on the ocean / vase of burning flowers / birds trying to drown out the sound of a fire engine

waste no time forget all about it

made perfect pancakes last night turned to ask what you thought of them before realizing you weren't here

she kisses the door after he walks out like a picture you don't ever remember having been taken of you / the doctor gave her a fistful of flowers from one of the bad paintings in his waiting room / he tried to call in dead but it didn't work the boss heard him breathing

the world turned on him like a child impatient to open new toys

you are the unhealthiest person I have ever met I really

admire that

a pet reading an encyclopedia

dirty white wall of my memory

he couldn't hear but could taste everything real well

midnight never lasts

a huge jet spelling my name in the sky with an orange crayon / money shatters like glass / freedom to do what you want isn't much freedom at all / feeling for the pulse of a sleeping friend / no wood no stove no fire

halo thunder

shadow of a plant on a wall looking like a bad haircut

hanging a piece of bread on her doorknob like a Do Not Disturb sign

can never think of a good enough reason to celebrate

just relax assume artistic control

he got his hands stuck inside his head and couldn't get them out

a man driving a car on a back road while reading a newspaper spread over the steering wheel / all you need is a little gasoline to get to America / reading Bridge May Be Icy signs through a windshield splattered with bird shit somewhere in Pennsylvania / born weak died weaker / flattened animal beside the highway like an abandoned rug looks like it wants to rise up and run home / clouds from childhood eating peanut butter and jelly sandwiches / the houses look afraid the way they're huddled together like that / bird feet touching down on naked branches / ninety-five miles to Columbus / sheep eating like razors as the sun takes down its hammock from between two trees to store in a barn on the other side of morning

this is more real to me than a lot of things / throw it away tear it up / sit as uncomfortably as possible at all times

he was afraid of his friends

Poesy County Indiana stunted wheat dismal corn / say your prayers even though they won't help / a three-person posse shooting at something in a tree in Omaha Illinois or was it Lincolnville Beach Maine he could no longer remember it could even have been Crystal River Florida for all he knew they don't even waste time making road signs around here / butterfly in the car window and then back out without saying a word

dumb and dangerous genes had already done enough damage for one lifetime

cold and tired not a single thought / he gave up young / see what any of it does for you / resist all forms of learning

she never reclaimed her mind because she never noticed it was missing

other people's decay inspired him / he hated himself to sleep at night / she made the bed each morning with her husband still in it

empty silo / recurring nightmare from childhood / nothing going on out there didn't see a thing after thousands of miles / for this we come to shore this very evening

never be alarmed by murder weapons found while cleaning the house

an unruly fetus in a full-mental body cast / grade school cop lurking in the hallway / just doing your job is no excuse for fucking people around

it helped pass the time he didn't see anything wrong with it

this is not the way it is done / every thought I have today makes me nauseous / trees dripping wax

he gave all his dealers bulletproof vests and 9mm guns

a parade out of focus blurry passing in the street / down the elevator to the grave

crumple up the sheets of paper / it didn't work I didn't work
it wasn't a good scene / your daisies are dying and so are you

bought a handgun in a dream felt like a pure menace to the
universe my finger on the trigger shiny metal short and heavy
I went outside and shot twice in the air

said I was leaving in the morning

she knew being dead meant no more dancing / sunlight on
the radio / blow-up dolls instead of scarecrows / don't shoot
anything I wouldn't shoot

New Bern North Carolina became a Mecca for him

a guy with a twenty-foot cigar just told me that I have the
perfect job he said you must read a lot I just smiled and nod-
ded I pretended I was mute it was easier that way I just sat
there like a broken sundial

the days fell into place like puzzles without pieces

the week before he had gotten a postcard from his dead grand-
mother in Corpus Christi so he wanted to stop in and see
her / a dog skeleton still awaiting ghost scraps under the table
/ blood dripping from the calendar

never hit the nail on the head no good will come of it ever
this sounds worse than it is

tattooing each other with ink from a pen and a safety pin /
her boyfriend was into downers she had to carry him home
at night like a child

someone had run into a telephone pole for their entertain-
ment / incoherent reportage / heard a woman crying on a pay
phone talking about her mother say they're going to keep
her as if the hospital staff now owned her

dusty bed near a broken window letting in fragments of light

he threw his best parts away smoking his memories next to a
cold radiator like a metal corpse his thoughts worth approxi-
mately two cents he wasn't sure whether he should run for
office or just run period off into the woods and never be seen
or heard from again he couldn't even fall down correctly
emptying an ashtray had gotten to be too much for him his
mind rusted shut with guilt fear hid its weapons in his eyes
but he still couldn't see the danger

nothing but words and more words this will get us nowhere

dada enigma loaded with verbal whiplashes stinging the
masses / a glutton for banishment

a burning birdhouse / wet paper smoking / slapping sounds
against the wall

he turned into himself at the slightest provocation

dust killed the plants

so few games left to play

Superman came from Smallville Illinois

the priest said do you take this man for worse than better
better than worse

lazy fuck with a lengthy excuse for each hour of the day /
send in the freaks forget it they're already here

some days I think there is something seriously wrong with
me and then the Lord will send me a little sign reminding
me that he made me in his image and since he isn't sick I'm
not either

there is cause for alarm / they promise the moon and give a
dog bowl

me and my several selves aren't talking to each other

slurred and incoherent speech

on Groundhog's Day he hired airplanes to skywrite Dear
Everyone in the World Will You Be My Valentine

a cloud fell onto the house with a crash but he didn't hear it

/ the TV didn't work but he watched it anyway because he didn't have a radio / a flying fish shed its watery clothing in a momentary effort to touch the sun falling several yards short / running for miles without taking a single step / we are all on the wrong team

prediluted dreams / a new territory admitted into the Union / Walt Whitman enters wearing a garbage man suit holding armloads of grass / distant dream city but visible intense reflection of sunlight on metal no reason to go there at all unless you are seriously ill like most people

a child on the Lower East Side pulling an old vacuum cleaner around as if it were a dog on a leash / shoot blood at the walls toss the spoon in the garbage / wearing devil horns the landlord bursts in has a fit with a seizure for good measure / missing all the signs / it's a long long story not sure it's worth telling but will anyway will and won't / stupid in a hurry / the right time never came / erect newspaper demanding a ride home / they got what they deserved / all is not well / decade-long argument / bright idea dim vision

leap year pizza / early screening of a bad film / all is said and done / rehearsed fainting spell / rusty edge of truth mistaken for a toy in Mt. Lemon Arizona Prison / the long end of the stick found out all about the short end bumping into each other in a wide-open field

tattooed at birth

never attend parties you've been invited to / blow it out of proportion / subtle osmosis dragged around by the collar / thinking in square circles of light

barefoot in a Japanese restaurant waiting for rice somewhere in Virginia / sad but untrue / monkey on one shoulder and a crow on the other / maybe those children were born right where they are on the side of the road

harbor no fear in your still heart

something happened somewhere / I'm not paying for any of this

a clock eating cigarette butts

please leave this alone put it back where you found it

cotton growing on the window

his favorite part about her eluded him

he was at a permanent loss / someday soon it will all come to an end / understanding will not save your soul / stone cold sober lucid but still couldn't make any sense / get used to it this is it sit back and relax refuse to get a grip on anything

mothers of Olympic athletes weeping on the TV

there is a revolution coming you had better take precautions if you want to be around to celebrate

too many TVs spoil the imagination

the best thing would be to forget about it

a baby pops like a grape its stomach bursts open with a gentle spurt of light brown gelatin and I cover your eyes because I don't want you to see it while you're driving the baby has webbed toes because it needs to use a water runway to fly it needs water to get to the sky

test everyone you know / it is written / you already look like yourself so don't change a thing / this is where the story ends / do not turn on the TV / the oldest penny in the jar / his watch prescribed the time to him like medication a wrist-band cure of sorts

pubic fetus on the corner of East 11th Street and Avenue A / he waited for eighteen years and nothing ever came to him

the TV reached over turned him off said out loud there is never anything good on the human anymore while an old notebook tied him up

the pitcher threw a body part at the unsuspecting batter there was nothing in the rule book that said he couldn't

the garden had a headache so he made it a cup of tea

her handbag was so complex that she had to give a blood sample every time she wanted to open it

a candle made of fur

the moon was full it had been eating all day

random thoughts ringing in his head like a bell filled with fake bats or a kingdom that evaporated in ice

then what happened

darkness echoing off the broken fingers of a blind pianist

he was on the fringe of the fringe

he sprang from bed like a drunken scarecrow began jumping up and down yelling I've found it I've found it went straight back to bed forgetting all about it

a camera devours dead histories / watching two pigeons kissing on a ledge / take this plastic trophy / dreams are free / the door is open

whenever the people downstairs bang on their ceiling he takes their daughter's bike with the training wheels still on and repeatedly rides it across the floor

I hate b-l-a-n-k written on the dead girl's baseball glove

gave it away for Christmas took it back on Groundhog's Day

he had been dead for a week but still kept leaving messages on his ex-girlfriend's machine / his most recent brainstorm was to start an encyclopedia of suicides through the ages / they were sitting around downstairs smoking and drinking with a few guests when they heard a tiny voice whispering helter-skelter over their four-month-old daughter's crib monitor / he dressed up as Santa Claus called the cops on himself and went into the cemetery and began digging in a random plot / his father got a job pumping gas because he loved the smell so much

a piece of hollow sacred ground

do what you like

there is no point in saving anything

he dreamed of champagne and caviar though he didn't like either

we thought a stranger had come over and died in the bathroom but it turned out to be someone we knew

no beginning or end

illegible scribbling / empty bird cage / children playing under the stars speaking in a dead tongue / cryptic scrawl about a ditch / a master of saying nothing entirely ignored / empty prison cells

the blank pages represented something

don't walk run / afraid to die / tow truck light flashing through the window hauling off the paper bag filled with your anatomy / went down to the river and drowned

too many memories on that couch / flea-infested dog shits its last leg through its nose / they conspired to get her goat and keep it

struck by thought lightning

fuck this this has gone on too long

hidden meanings was their thing

his feet grew feet and walked away / stolen car ashtray filled with marked bills / a vision holster around his waist / soul-invading parasites / his dream came true but killed him as soon as it did / bleeding to death in the hospital waiting room / watching television murdering hours / the steering wheel came off in his hands while in the passing lane / the sun scared away all the mud puddles / her limo had the nuclear option / police searched the car all they found was a branding iron / one-hundred-year-old man on a motorcycle

his mind was a cheap imitation but he treated it as if it were a signed original

parking meters deep in the woods / the guys at the garage couldn't help change the flat tire in his head / Cerberus the three-headed dog of hell is sitting on the porch wanting to get in

there were two brothers one wanted to be president the other to be the general manager of the local crematorium

lightning striking a wagon over a hundred years ago

the quicker you say good-bye the better

his car was so fast you never saw it you had to take his word for it that it was nice

this is poison do not read this

New York New Jersey Mississippi Massachusetts Texas

my brain if it is still legal to call it one is a socket occupied by a telephone call made before the ice age / turn all of it off don't call back / clouds over a motel like blankets covering napping infants the clouds would rather be sleeping in the motel themselves but can't because they are working / X marks the nothing / they decided to keep it because they knew it would come in handy someday

tabloid article about a woman who lost so much weight that she no longer exists

finger paint all over the walls / a waterfall driving a linen closet

he'd forget his hat if it weren't sewn on

tap-dancing with cinder blocks affixed to his feet / a fish with hair staring at itself in the mirror with repulsion / vapor in a dream woven through a sewing machine / better to be a weather vane or a bird than to be this

he felt like a ground mole with wings made from an old note to himself / the radiant afterglow began its oratory whatever that means / we're sorry we can't complete your call / he was all pinkies / he gathered up his verbal nonsense and put it back in his mouth / he could tie his shoes while falling down the stairs you had to see it to believe it

there was an abstraction in the toolbox where a wrench should have been

pitch-black inside an incinerator of straw cowboy hats

flash bulb flashes on an ice cube

diseased Christmas lights strung like dead birds on the side of a stucco house

a coincidence fell on him crushed him to death

one of the guests arose from the table to use the bathroom and proceeded to demolish it with a ten-pound sledgehammer he split the toilet and sink in half broke the mirror and smashed every inch of sheetrock came back out and calmly sat back down at the table as if nothing out of the ordinary had happened

the fine print of his own thoughts fucked him over in a mental court of law / he ripped himself off for a lot worse than money

damp leaves crashing to the ground like silverware / safes filled with celestial pool balls

undeveloped pictures from childhood

he locked himself in his room for twenty years watching his fingernails grow waiting for them to get long enough to chew off again / the radioactive mattress made his hair fall out / they drew the bucket from the well and it had a palpitating human heart in it

he was standing in front of a shop window which had a holo-
gram of Jesus that blinked when you looked at it when a
psycho asked him what he wanted to which he replied noth-
ing and kept talking to his friend the psycho went and leaned
against a wall to stare menacingly at him until suddenly squar-
ing off in front of him with two extended fingers stopping a
few inches from his eyes saying with his I coulda just poked
out yer motherfucking eyes white boy

sink the Niña the Pinta and Santa Maria before Columbus
has a chance to land

Bubblegum Horoscope

Can you make no use of nothing, nuncle?
—William Shakespeare, *King Lear*

hail in the microwave / an elephant crawling into a tuba in the midst of the ghosts of one hundred classical composers / draw back the bow randomly release arrows at no particular target

an unmeasured equator / angry trains run on their own schedules

do the people that die on the news really exist or do they fake their deaths just to get on TV

a gnome carved him a wooden tombstone / a souvenir piece of lava on the mantel / he wanted to have a ghostwriter but wondered who would hold the pen for it

the birthday boy refused to play games with the other children acting like the one pilgrim that didn't get along with the others and ate alone that historic first Thanksgiving

an apple with a core made of the minimum wage / tied to the attention span of a fractured ego / tied to the first steps taken in space / using a mop to split electrons

I didn't see your face in the snow at all this winter

an abandoned house falling in on itself / light spilling sound out of the pores of a mountain like smoke inside a marble / a suitcase filled with burnt toast he puked blood in his cereal bowl and put a cigarette out on his neck near the jugular vein he pissed on his lung and skull X-rays in the bathtub he went out for a walk dragging an old doll on a rope

black tar poured over the wigs in aisle four bursting into flames / the pond dried up all the fish thought they had done something wrong / all the buildings in town ejected their elevators through the roof everyone began using the stairs again / he was a hostage to his mailbox had to check it at least a hundred times a day

sitting on a green bench in Tompkins Square Park in front of an empty methadone container / blue sky at night / people sleeping in tents in the dead of winter dogs on leashes people standing around fires in wire garbage pails neon signs police sirens car horns cold teeth homeless old men tougher than any of us sitting around

lightning aggressively wrestling with the sky

he never forgot that at the end of *Brave New World* the savage hangs himself

overwhelming pressure to finish the moat / bruised moss / light bulb dangling in a cave like a key to a nonexistent lock

these words will not launch a rocket / tear up the guidelines a stray thought made a mad dash from the herd and was lassoed like a bird in a reptile's clothes / buried an empty time capsule in the yard

can't be certain of anything / mean what you say if you can

the cows don't like you they have their faces pressed against the dining room window watching you eat a steak / if looks could kill you would have been dead a long time ago / tied to a chair in the yard trying to alert the neighbors was her strong point / someone was letting the phone ring for hours / a cadaver with insomnia has an epiphany / kept getting the same letter from her over and over she kept writing the same thing and mailing it from different parts of the country

they cut his oxygen line but he still wasn't coming up he'll have to come up soon for a cigarette the first mate said to the impatient grocer making a fireplace out of a train wreck sailing across photographs of cows

cancer walked right out of him and heaped itself up in the corner like a rug that had seen a ghost

a new muffler for the camel / grass growing like hair / he was dull to the point of being interesting they were teaching him how to become a statue at a public landmark / the old jailhouse laughing like a hyena on ether / mushrooms growing on lopsided clouds under the house / a monk in the synagogue reading her mail it has been proven living causes cancer

some old weather in a shoe box

forever is a long long time

pitchforks of the sun poking us with rays / a cherry tree strangled by a butter churn

there is no sense like no sense

an insect rubbing its hands together greedy for the entire sky / halo-robber / shoot the TV Elvis-style / burned-up love letters dropping in water like a kite tied to a wedding accidentally dragging it off toward the sky / rainwater evaporating your smile into a memory / light glittering on tombstones like a head of cattle ringing in a church bell like roses burning on a battlefield

half-eaten thinking caps

they flipped a coin to choose which of two roads to take skipping off down the road to peril and eternal perdition hand in hand

a comet in a green chariot rushing past the window

the shovel was much too happy-looking so they made it dig a

hole and buried it

the pigeons are grouped around like religious sects / the man at the end of the bench is either mesmerized by a tabloid article or is having some sort of flashback because his face is twitching and his eyes are bulging

a plaque that reads this tablet marks the land upon which stood Four Chimneys the house occupied by General George Washington as headquarters during the battle of Long Island in which the Council of War was held August 29th 1776 when it was decided to withdraw the American Army from Long Island

temporarily on fire

he was talking to his Siamese twin on the phone / new laws made everything illegal / it will all become a dream soon enough

dyed his hair white and wrote a letter to his ex-wife that would surely estrange her forever

a butterfly net dangling from a flag flying at half-mast / drunkenly falling on the exhibit / a perfume well in the yard / memory erased like a blackboard / a man walking toward you with several feet of his own intestine on a tray

the cat behaved like a fire engine

a crude camera made out of a few rocks and a wilted flower for a flash bulb

you're all alone this time like everyone else kid

tea in a coffee cup / feeling faint and up to the challenge like the stocks and bonds of a man dead for an hour / space dust in an urn / a sperm whale with a mane setting fire to the water bed / sitting at a table at midnight chain-smoking cigarettes with two cats staring through the window / it was October and the leaves were still green the townspeople were shooting the leaves off with shotguns the smaller children leveled bb guns at the trees

wanna haveta needta seemta gotta hopeta aspireta meanta

blame me for everything

desolate cabin / in a Jeep / half a pack of some cigarettes a radio playing a TV show

assume artistic control

seasonal parking in hell

drinking with the saints on the terrace / a mop strand dangling from an electrical cord near the ceiling who knows how it got there

he could hold his breath for weeks / the stream was running
from something but would never say just what / he received
an invitation to the wedding they just didn't tell him where
it was he was welcome to try and find it on his own but they
knew he wouldn't

playing golf in three feet of snow when a vulture swooped
down snatched his imagination and flew off with it / hands
passing through a rainbow

he brought an ax to the picnic which made everyone ner-
vous / she placed an ad that said can't remember what I lost
but I know I'm missing something if you find anything please
call or write

a hired cliché-hunter at the door

she read a lot the only trouble was it was always the same
page over and over thousands of times

nothing is sacred

clutter reduced him to psychotic fits

heated swimming pool installed in a cave / walking across a
floor of razor blades toward a check for one million dollars / a
radio that only picked up perverse folk music from forgotten
cultures / unsigned original flesh paintings

no time unlike the present

wind eroding ice / an umbrella dated with a Magic Marker / a submarine periscope breaking through the sidewalk / all he had in the world were his tattoos and scars / a dramatic death flop / the mad leading the mad / a dog barking in a city street like a paper bag colliding with tumbleweed on a dirt floor

kneeling at the Indian child's grave removing the fallen branches

find things before they find you be ready for them

looking in the suitcase of the sky to find airplanes folded like socks clouds like favorite shirts / the bronco got a higher score than its rider

avoiding authority figures became a vocation

insects with degrees in bloodsucking

she quit smoking and bought a small religious cult with the money she saved / he had a gift certificate for immortality but was afraid to cash it in / they closed the bowling alley jailed the bowling balls the village idiot declared martial law

an electrical outlet in a colonial home

a raindrop went swimming / a fence circled around a misunderstanding / air inside a jar being taunted by air on the outside / snow ascending back into the sky / a Neanderthal waiting for his water to boil in the microwave

a painting of a clown without a face

generic tar pit

blind men looking through telescopes / a house with no doors or windows / crazy three-legged cat in the rain limping toward cover / lead flags at half-mast / an elephant dead in a mousetrap

in the last episode our hero was dangling from a suspension bridge about to fall to his death when the screen went blank

the newspaper read him inside out threw him away with the junk mail / the little things were what pushed him over the edge / a meteorological posse wielding lassos of lightning / tree-lined lane somewhere in southern California / he heard a stick of butter say something to him and promptly checked into a rehab

you needed a space shuttle to get to the front desk of the motel

a beard riding a motorcycle solo it used a mustache to hold the handlebars

peeling paint broken radios crying out in unison no good will come of it

the clouds looked like the stolen art treasures that Napoleon was forced to return / next stop Grand Army Plaza / pigeons dragging their shadows around like balls and chains

an egg regaining consciousness

a table for two for three people / a simple solution to the most difficult questions

a confetti junkyard

he enjoyed pouring lemon juice in his paper cuts / he fully intended to waste his life / no time to waste

every slice of bread was a heel

thousands of just-in-case dollars in the bank

East collided with West and North with South wherever you needed to be you were already there

two glass hammers smashing fruit / wet park bench sun creeping around the sky like a soggy tombstone riding the horse of irony / an egg with no shell / skin-removing soap / arithmetic famine / butterflies passing by like notebooks opening and closing / a birthday cake made with raw fish it seemed strange for the fingerprints he left on a postcard to be in Florida without him

an anvil stuffed inside a thimble / baited mousetraps on the ceiling / a stick looking like a snake / a paper hut in a monsoon / a painting stuck in a spider web

the landfills of America / two hundred years late for the gold rush mining away regardless finding nothing / another ice age impending a glacier melting in the living room

dear diary was all she could get down before closing the book

without missing a beat the conductor shot and killed the cellist who played a wrong note

rusty nails driven into slices of white bread on the picnic table / a slug the size of a small car

the sign said Don't Walk so the pigeon looked both ways and flew across the street / a man at the counter drinking coffee through a straw in his nose

two-foot-wide eye peering in the window

his favorite particle ran away from home / a fingerprint running away from the scene of the crime / cop in the subway car about six feet four inches tall standing about five feet four inches away stares at me as I write him a ticket

sun behind a cloud choking on its luminous medicine / dissension in the ranks / he held the fort in the palm of his hand if anyone attacked he had orders to just make a fist

even the part-time stars are out tonight / seventeen thousand mummies fishing under a small bridge

just forget it / they promised if she died during winter that they would dig her a grave so she wouldn't be stored in the morgue until spring / your guardian angel called again this morning his secretary told him

the world ended when he switched on the light / building a snowman on the beach / obscure opera played on instruments that no longer exist / the airport sending its metal laundry into the sky filled with plenty of change for the dryers / clouds recognized from childhood / Mt. Cobb Pennsylvania houses clustered together as if afraid of something churches and road signs blue sky and sunshine

parking tickets of the dead

twenty-four-hour dust

pigs wearing shoes in church / dirt-blackened feet

a child trying to put the entire Atlantic Ocean in his squirt gun / sunbathers turning their chairs 15° an hour like human sundials / dreams rolling onto shore / a meaningless white dish rack / cars dripping up some highway in Queens like a leaky faucet / shattered bills of money / one thousand shitty movies stuck in her head

someone in a tree wearing an Afro wig made of fiberglass insulation

they say the average housefly can fly five miles per hour

this is for the birds this is for their wings not mine for their feet to land on branches not mine

get wild be crazy while you can

woman lying in her coffin with curlers in her hair / swan floating majestically down a polluted river dunking its head in the mire like a puppet

stars filling the boats of the sky with fishy light / TV on all night playing static for a lemon-colored black cat

in a car getting closer to Memphis as Elvis gets deader / we just don't know any better like a swimming bird or a fish making a crude nest in a tall tree

reading a blank road map at Twelve Forks in the Road / a mirror wedged in between two garbage cans / a lampshade driving a stolen pink stucco car to a library leveled by an earthquake sitting around waiting for small eroded particles to gather themselves together and transform into sedimentary rock made him 200 million years late for the party

his boat hated the water his beach hated the sand / show off your best side when and if you find it

a significant study showed nothing

dirt under the fingernails / writing lyrics to Hank Williams songs on infants

the spider returned to its web and found another spider's reflection in its mirror / the morning mail never came again

4th Avenue crawling with insect-like yellow taxis and limos longer than the geologic time line / where were you on the night of July 3rd 1872 the lawyer asked him on the witness stand I was born in 1978 that's no excuse that's not what I asked you the lawyer shouted back slamming his hand on the table / fire tearing through the wilderness like hot scissors smoldering house perfume lingering on a fireman's clothes / he had a tooth pulled today and can't eat has been left with a swollen face looks like he's hoarding golf balls in his mouth

froze to death in the desert / a woodpecker tearing into a globe / coming in loud and clear who would be here in my place if I weren't me / Edison stole Franklin's kite and got it higher / the Great Wall of China crashing through the walls of a theater near you / a knock on a door in the mind like a magic trick that never worked

he sold his soul for a leaf blower / he could never get a picture of nature without power lines in the way

four women overheard in Manhattan one evening I don't enjoy it anymore five or six German accents how do I get to 121st Street sometimes you just go too far

a draft running freely through the house / held in the arms of silence / shadow of a flea on the wall

a cattle prod posing as a leather jacket / Elvis singing a George Harrison song on TV / the reflection of a hermit's eyes on paper / I hated what was written on that piece of paper so I threw it away

he stopped talking offered no explanation like a message in a bottle dancing around the room without feet

a traced hand on a notebook cover

I'll be right over

a female cop on the subway with her head turned sideways making faces at a baby in a stroller with the happiest parents in the city a man was sleeping on a bench at the next stop and the cop shook her head in disgust

the wind made the cabin creak like amplified bones

he was sitting at the counter waiting for a second cup of coffee the waitress noticed and was slowly making her way toward him we will leave them both there

The Unknown Soldier late for the party / tumbleweed blowing across a field of bowling balls / riding a wobbly-wheeled tricycle on a heap of garbage / fish-scale glitter like the bird on a long stick in the cave paintings at Lascaux / an invisible kite guarded by a decomposing watchdog incapable of warding off even insects

a single-prong fork / abandoned toys in a cemetery / an animal taking its first steps

great titles horrible poems

beating on stumps with an ax was his art form

crow jumping into the woods like a black ghost leaping off the bridge landing on a guardrail like a shotgun-blasted kite

he was never going to work for the government buy a car vote fix a sink own property or stocks eat meat wear a suit join the army have life insurance kill anyone own a home be a priest live in New Jersey be a doctor or lawyer or cop plant a tree be famous catch a fish testify in a court of law pay taxes eat an egg be on TV dig a ditch slip in the shower have a business card or car phone fly a plane have a face-lift have his initials on towels or clothing be a bartender have animal heads on the walls win any trophies get any medals join a union live in a trailer park wear a watch give blood get healthy be reincarnated strike oil see a UFO gamble wear ugly hats grow a gray beard be taken hostage be buried in Arlington be ten years old again join the NRA count calories stand at attention he was never going to hijack an airplane skin a deer steal second base pencil on eyebrows dance beg sue anyone be president of a large corporation dress up on Halloween wear a party hat on New Year's Eve build a bomb shelter die in bed get a hunting license be thrown a parade christen a boat paint a mural speak in tongues flip his wig fall down stairs have a two-car garage have children

a field of cows ignoring the UFO hovering above them they just weren't interested / his goat was shot out from underneath him / cornhusks grew from his back / clouds with their hands tied behind their backs

"Something Simple Made Difficult" was her middle name

18th-century headstones beside a rarely traveled country road a two-year-old boy dead two hundred years is closest to the waist-high entrance gate

the most creative days he would ever have had already eloped with his thoughts like the skin of an onion that fell from a star / ready for brisk walks through fallen leaves / photo of an apple on the vine of a grape tree

saw a woman's one-piece bathing suit covering a fire hydrant in the Lower East Side taken off by a homeless guy who held it up in front of himself to see if it would fit beggars can't be choosers as they say later in the day I saw him wearing it around over his clothes / he was chasing his exhaled smoke about the room

roots of dead hair sewing socks together / an ugly duckling in a shopping cart / raw numbers gave her the horrors / beating dead horses for a living / tears welling in his glass eye / there is dust on the TV / pulling papers out of his pocket and burning them

she was hugged by trees on sunshine acid during the Summer of Love / he began smoking in the womb even had his own ashtray / his arm was deformed so he took it out on his dogs / he used to paint but after his house burned down with all his work in it he couldn't bear to continue

yellowed newspaper clippings on the wall / now it all makes sense like a picture you have already taken and placed in a frame

people starting cars going off to work some to notice that their license plates have been stolen a street lamp using chopsticks a plastic wishbone trying to write a poem / wholesale genius / plastic people clapping in studio audiences / wounded kites on windless days / his dreams didn't have any punctuation / the reflection of power lines in your sunglasses / tin-can trees / two blurry photographs / Eve split Eden without paying Adam for the rib cage / widows of war veterans slowly walking down the street

an arm needing a hand a face needing skin

a phone rings in a trailer in Toledo Oregon but isn't answered / protesting alone in the rain with a sign that said Everything Sucks / singing love songs through shattered windows laughing when nothing is funny / a homeless man passed out under the Welcome to Washington DC sign on a patch of grass with a big bottle of wine next to him in a paper bag

glass doorknobs / violent destruction / read yourself drunk

a woman in an elevator asked me if I was a Rolling Stone not yet I said

bullheads in a bucket inside a leaky canoe

his story had no moral no point like a void with a bubble in it

keep in touch with what you hate

ghosts of children using the swings without permission / ten blades of cattail grass clapping their bodies together like frantic hands rushing across an empty blue stage as the flag in the park lazily wraps itself around a white flagpole / a stranger handing out birth certificates / same old faces doing saying the same old things / names people are no longer called

the librarian's ink stamps have dried up and blown away like sagebrush / blue eyes that can almost see to Iowa / burning a glass of water / sun gone behind a cloud realizing its childhood is missing / the van had no tires so they stopped going anywhere

among the lucky you are the chosen one

headaches for breakfast / a pay phone ringing in the rain / Remember the Alamo Save the Whales / falling flat on his face trying to bid at an auction while in a coma he exploded into a million sleeping pieces

stuffing a grape in a snorkel / a red fire hydrant in a grove of peach trees / the clock stopped like a kite out of string like a moth slipping on the soap in the shower

they shot the horse in the starting gate before it had a chance to break its leg

a picture in flames within its frame / wind blowing through a keyhole no alarm could stop it / a haystack smelling a pitchfork / sitting on a chair of nails / wrestling his mattress as if it

were an alligator with springs for teeth / trying to murder a
bullet in the garage / pink flamingo voodoo doll

maybe we should be suspicious of you have you investigated

stale daily bread / putting two and two together coming up
with nothing

meat-cleaver curtains

the child tore up his exam and made an elaborate paper castle
with it / haunted hallways / a decomposed parrot wrapped in
newspaper in a shoe box in the cellar / he limped through
the door of the city like a self-contained swamp monster

the Invisible Man on money

three visible stars the rest were devoured by the lights of the
skyline / couples walking by arm in arm waiting to be struck
by something like hot spaghetti on the neck

they painted the White House hot pink

shot by a deer in the woods / walking on stilts in a crowd of
dwarfs / as a child playing hide-and-seek he once disappeared
for a week

a thought crawling a corridor of his mind

orange peels on the sidewalk a biodegradable littering ticket / children so small that the wind blew them away

Jell-O in a toothless mouth

shuffle your intelligence like a deck of cards

rounds later he'd forgotten where he was

an infant tearing down an old house

a paper bag and some crayons

he just doesn't give a fuck so you can't count on him

a bed of nails hatching cotton balls into green thumbs / a skeleton of a light bulb relaxing in a chair / tiny sheep swirling down a sink drain

the TV went dead at the bar during the big game and everyone killed themselves in the parking lot

opening a can of worms to let them breathe a little

what time is it he asked it's now the man walked away confused

I just found this piece of paper under a chair and quickly

snatched it up and wrote this on it

an inside for the outside

an elephant trunk on a flea / a body arriving at the morticians already embalmed / firemen burning everything down cops stealing anything in sight / your favorite newscaster calling you names on the air

he pulled his own head off because the pictures on the wall were crooked

he broke his own bones spilled his own guts on the floor put himself in his own coffin wrote a note to whom it most likely doesn't concern

heads I win tails you lose

swinging a golf club at a gasoline piñata / an embryo wearing a wig / he was beyond the repair of any handyman in any trade / the baby's mobile was a pot holder on a coat hanger / he started seeing whales everywhere after he was run over by a child named Melville riding a white bike carrying a copy of *Moby Dick*

the artless hands of nature made a mess of her

easily overlooked like that last crumb hiding on a piece of dirt / too much red in the flag their house shriveled up like an old balloon / starving cats under the porch chewing on cans / she wanted to go to the store but didn't need anything she made a list with nothing on it

incorrect historical dates in old diaries

pacing himself to death he wondered if he had thrown away the best parts of himself without noticing because there certainly wasn't much left / working at forgetting / wheezing like a coyote but chain-smoking anyway / the spirit of America was sending him hate mail / they fired him before he even got the job

nothing is my favorite word

a burn next to a scar / pink cars parked in the snow

sweating out his fear onto a pile of broken promises

he was a prophet but he wasn't

instant fossils just add water / tears shattering like windows

the pencil tried to pretend it was filled with ink but no one fell for it

a city burning to the ground in a mirror

the pilgrims should have stayed home / watching a Christmas movie in July / the huge watery eye of the Atlantic winked at me / sun sizzling into the sky's frying pan like a fried egg / the Mayflower should have sunk

she was in love with a ghost

fallen leaves hopping down the street in potato sacks / shotgun holes in the sky

reading the paper and looking in the mirror were the same thing to him

drastically limited options / just keep breathing

the storm came unexpectedly the snow didn't even know it was falling / stolen gloves keeping a stranger's hands warm

it gets a little closer everyday

ghosts tracking mud all over the floor

elephant-crossing

the morning fit like customized skin / the ocean heard its name being called

tragedy fell in the castle

bloody heads rolling in the street like deranged marbles

homeless guys in front of the McDonalds on West 4th Street wearing paper bags on their heads on Halloween / a million years later the subscription ran out like fishing line messages floating at sea like missing children

step right this way folks / once saw an old-timer with a bluefish and I ran right up to it he told me to be careful showed me his hand where he was missing two fingers they bite kid / a 1972 quarter to make a 1986 phone call / she's not as old as she looks / fake seagulls on string in the sky

two crippled virgins borrowing money from a blind priest / a frozen light bulb / outlets with fish heads stuffed in them / the past pieces itself back together / tombstones in a race to the finish

it's the thought that counts but not for much / he had a chance as long as there were no sounds other than his own in the room

animals shadowboxing in the forest / is this happening is this real / entering Arkansas a speed limit sign says No Tolerance / a fish gnawing on a cat / acres of New York City garbage / a sign nailed to a tree in Virginia that said Jesus Is Coming Soon

the carpet speaks French the front porch only understands

Dutch the fireplace was reared in Belgium the doorbell rings
in Spanish the toaster makes toast in German the couch and
I speak English

endless litany of missed moments ingrained pattern of abuse

it was fair to partly partly out

hitting the hay with clenched fists

a lighthouse reading a bedtime story to the boats in the bay
/ multiple-choice trivia questions flashing on the scoreboard
the horde screaming the answers into space

doomed from beginning to end

bad bad writing

he should have gotten paid for making a fool of himself he
would have been rich / skeletons don't eat much / the powers
that be are ugly / the shepherd of interpretations was caught
sleeping on the job

he made one demand of his friends that they sneak up be-
hind him with a hammer and kill him if he became one of
them

the baby sitter could tell the kids horror stories just by look-
ing at them / once upon a time there was very little which

turned into even less

hold onto this for me until I get back I won't be long try and make yourself comfortable wait now that I think of it forget it I'm never coming back

saving souls and giving up hope / getting by with little

short walk off a long pier / a small town filled with junk mail / chickens in the living room watching TV / a ghost wearing a sheet for a joke / it makes a big difference whatever it is / he had nothing and nowhere to put it / relying on the radio as a crutch / the best he could do wasn't even close / John Wayne drunk in *True Grit* falling off his horse we're camping here right here / frozen eleven-year- old image on the TV / a lasso like a snake swallowing its tail

they never asked him if he had a last request

am I on yet was all she could say

they named their first-born Elvis Hitler Manson

wolf-fish / half-way to the Promised Land

much too late to be early / coming in a stranger going out even stranger

wet leaves stuck to the highway like flattened starfish / a large rip in the side of the desert / complex vapors sunk their teeth into the seashore / plastic eggs on the brink of extinction

reading by the light of an ugly lamp / seasons changing like drawers opening and closing / a single boat bobbing like a cork / nothing but memories

it took decades to grow and a few minutes to cut down

save your words like mental piggy bank coins / cutting through tangled nightmares / long shot in the dark / streets filled with tables / upside-down mountains / an insect ballet / a skyscraper sprouting from the ground in a dense forest

he washed his hands of it but they were still as dirty as before / had his spine removed to help his art / reenacting the Great Flood with an unemployed bus driver playing Noah / an open door foreboding black clouds

writing with the left hand

flowers crying themselves to sleep / a bale of hay cleaning its young behind the pickup truck / the cows were lured to the stream in a catatonic state / a pond on a frog / a tunnel in your feet walking you home / plaid sperm cells under the microscope / a farm on the head of a pin

she went to lick the envelope but it pulled out a switchblade and cut her tongue off

sitting in a boat in the yard / he had the laugh of a wise man but he was a fool

a skeleton trying to find work

it kept getting easier to put things off

leaves falling upward never landing never seen again / trees slowly forming wings / a car key starting a dead fish / trading teeth for whiskey / a flag a tire a halo some string and a cow / blind dog climbing a ladder

eat this note

a lamp plugged into the ground beside a grave

a pancake tree

she says one thing and then does ten others so as not to be predictable

a reminder on the fridge not to have the dog stuffed yet / taking two more of his dog's tranquilizers

writing hokku in Dale Indiana haiku in Tennessee / lines of the road endless towns barely on the map / birds using string to flap plastic and leather wings through the open air / Madison County garden freshwater lake firewood neatly stacked on a brick porch tall thin pine trees barns for lawn ornaments

Exxon Mobil daydreaming at dusk / a leaf caught like food spinning in a flimsy spider web

spend more time in hell

dead butterfly on the sidewalk with the wind still flapping its wings

it was always Mardis Gras in his head

he knew exactly everything and nothing

America is a big dumb dangerous place

day after night night after day

the sound of a pine tree wincing in flames

tying off with his umbilical cord to mainline 40 ccs of Drano

blank newspapers / a broken wagon / all the lights are out / he wrote a column for the *Daily Travesty* / the wind blowing him into her thoughts

the doctor jumped down his throat to check his tonsils

snowballs biodegrading like a memory

seeing the wrong signs

even if he's dead he'll be getting up soon

tired of saying how great everything is

a girl named Heather just walked by with a praying mantis in her hand / no light anywhere near the tunnel

he had work to do but didn't believe in any of it

bark on the trees guarding books to be published in the future / the syntax and punctuation furthermore throw the perception out of focus / words buried in an atomic coffin / he wore his plaid pants pulled up to his eyelids / clay death mask six feet below the ground

calmly say no don't ask questions / talking with his hands which are no more than tickets to the proper words / a mile-long want list

the best cops are the ones you never see

keep it for as long as forever lasts

won't need a room

no stranger to repetition / first things last / days spent and respent / a picnic table just coughed / the killer called grotesquely prolific in an old magazine / a Poe story

cement fields of honey

the kids burned the firehouse down just to be able to say they did something bad

the world will eat her in one dainty little bite

it was all a joke but no one ever caught on

a man driving down 7th Avenue in Park Slope with the tiniest Chihuahua I've ever seen on his shoulder / a life-size voodoo doll of Elvis

he lost his taste in a card game / he had a gallery show of his personal demons

buildings filled with ghosts / hello sucker welcome to life

a statue bathed in purple light looking in the closet for lost pieces of itself / a circus clown stretched out on a medieval rack / a flower wearing tennis sneakers running away from a swarm of bees / his face no longer fit his skull properly so he had it taken off / a black heart painted on a loaded gun / blank pages hurt his eyes so he felt compelled to fill them with nonsense

American flag contact lenses on all the eyes / smoke in his veins / black roses at graveside / hollow sparklers in the hands of children held out of dismal Brooklyn windows on the 4th of July

she fell down but didn't want to get back up so they put a fence around her and made an instant zoo / his inner child hung himself in the womb / the magic is lost deconstruct it don't bother putting it back together / there is no order chaos is master

they shot glue in his veins to hold him together for a few more days

glad to be so uninvolved / psychic jukebox / fuck it already

insane words spit them out / lost gone forever empty

getting off the train at Grand Central Station the train conductor says over the public address welcome to Dodge City you lucky devils stay alert and stay alive / ugly day with no money / silly girl living in a real-life soap opera asking what should we do about it into a silent phone / hope it holds up in a court of law

getting back together again for no apparent reason

a personalized nowhere

sew your mouth closed do us a favor

deadline madrigal / red white and blue paranoia / two crows
fly off like magnets learning how to use silverware

home again for the night in a strange motel room seized by
the unholy spirit he began preaching for hours under an over-
pass in Hernando Mississippi after the police tried to set him
up behold ye are of nothing wash this out of your life the
sermon confused the children / taking the tour of Graceland
listening to the guides lie

trapped in a stagnant present

already here tickets please next stop will be nowhere tickets

green trees driving in circles in the parking lot / wings rotting
underground

the chicken crossed the road to get the hell away from all the
people / a screeching wail of guitar feedback / a dead dog
that looks stuffed / real live buffalo out the car window

adversary nocturnal coterie

empty wire trees dirty patches of snow silos road signs bill-
boards tire marks bales

umbrellas lobsters sailboats rafts seagulls / a jet made of

laughter / the sky switched off like a memory / setting sail on a journey to his soul with no boat passing piles of monkey carcasses and heaps of old magazines and tires

born strange ending up in a state of complete weirdness / climbing up his own balcony to serenade himself with some stupid song he wrote / mailing postcards to crows general delivery

negative pennies held up to the light and shot full of holes / fending off ugly memories

monster on the drag strip / run and hide

children getting contact highs from a coat hanger

rabbits squirrels birds a dead raccoon

cold plastic dreams evaporating into black vinyl collecting boring thoughts and channeling them

he was a full-time degenerate death knocked at the door and he let it in like a fool

burning each other like wood / no tunnel no light / stolen moments in borrowed rooms / send money immediately there is no time to elaborate

they put the genie back in the bottle and buried it under the house / she wore blinders to the supermarket

he couldn't get a ride from the womb to the Post Office to mail copyright forms so much of his best work was stolen while he was still a fetus

pieces of buildings taped to some low clouds behind the Brooklyn Bridge

stars squinting to read over people's shoulders

they stole his identity and he didn't want it back

sending smoke signals to a dead father / a fish falling through the sky / a bee the size of a small dog passes by / later never came

she's on the train about a week ago going back to a meeting she's already been to remaking the presentation

a lab rat sued the federal government on the grounds of general abuse and won / a hippie and a Marine got married while going over Niagara Falls in a barrel

a cigarette sunrise / precious knowledge spilling out a hole in the side of her head disappearing like balloons without strings

a goatee on a sperm cell / sprinkling soup mix over a brick

let the lost remain lost

cut down like a toy tree / he thought the car was a horse so he piled rocks in front of it to keep it from getting away

be thankful that no one calls the law / trade it all in for a clue / they set the tent up in the house because they didn't know how to camp and didn't want to get in over their heads

a light bulb floating in the pond / a swan eating dirt and bugs in the woods / a mask on the flamingo / it all dwindled away / his funeral was held at the local landfill / dogs chained to a still life of an empty meat locker / step right this way leave your skeleton at the door

a doctor losing his practice in a hand of poker

the building tied him up in knots

she hopes the thunderstorm comes right to their front door

did I tell you about the pig I met at the church picnic

the brain of the candle melted it can no longer think about burning / the street lamp is an envelope of light ripped open above parked cars

the hands of the clock chasing each other around

it's been a pleasure but not really / attention shoppers aisle ten is now open for your convenience

she turned into someone else and no one recognized her anymore / she was so boring that phone booths used to walk away from her

pine cones crashing to the ground / miracle onion skin / bird nests filled with snow / rusty locomotives / three red curtains in a window across the way

a teenager carrying around his invisible luggage

haunted carpet in the beehive

throwing his life away one piece at a time

a crow like a stranger in a black sombrero walks against traffic as if hitchhiking like a fingerless hand and a glove that fits it perfectly / North America playing gun games in the woods of childhood / hands in the air like kites tangled in trees / firemen in the trees pretending to rescue invisible cats / pedants and serial killers hitchhiking down a one-way dead-end street

ironic decay / foreground action / recycling Confucius / headache like a grocery store filled with rotten fruit / a reflection of an American flag rippling with wind in a mud puddle outside the post office her bubblegum horoscope said the next two years of your life will be profitable

homicidal child thinking unpleasant thoughts / he carried many crosses / serving time in a mental hell / a projector chewing film like thread piecing together a plot

trading vitamins for a totem pole / a pancake on a breakfast table in the sky above an afterthought / a board propped against a building with the word flamingo on it

worn out welcome on their wedding day / wait one minute while I take a phone call / the moths take off their bodies like clothing and take a shower / young blades of grass hitch-hiking south for the winter / conversation tunneling like moles through the phone lines scaring all the birds off the wire

he lost his finger over the Bermuda Triangle as he ran it over a map as if it were an imaginary airplane piloted by Amelia Earhart

hair nets reenacting the conference at Yalta / a coat hanger holding a jacket as if it had hands / a bee lost its shirt and began selling Avon products flower to flower / a steel wool cop pulled a frying pan over in the sink asked to see its license and registration in the closet a broom was trying to sell a mop a used car while the mop was trying to get up the nerve to ask the vacuum for a date a spaceship landed on second base during the double-header they did their best to play around it

just looking out the window talking to a notebook

the atmosphere evicted the water cycle for not paying rent

he said I'm in the city all right see you tomorrow and hung up the pay phone on the corner of Bleeker and Sullivan and then he walked away

sewing together a ton of bricks / an interplanetary pincushion stole the show

plastic birds eating rubber worms / breeze stirring the shadows like soup

blah blah blah

a Venus Fly Trap eating light bulbs on a small stage / sitting on the speed of light going nowhere fast / a family eating the upholstery of their car at the drive-in

he drove into Kentucky and turned right around and went back to Tennessee / looking around like a dog seeking its master

fear crept in like mice began nibbling away at the cheese in her head footprints of town drunks in the cement of Main Street like a mini-Sunset Boulevard / an idiot staring back at him in the mirror

they thought their dog was possessed so they called in a faith-healer to lay hands on it

riding a silver spoon around town

the penal code came in soaking wet and shook itself off all over the dog sleeping on the rug by the fireplace

whatever it is that you want get it for yourself get on with it so we can go home

he was trying to commit suicide with a bb gun / a child maimed by a bad dream

they don't get it

swans on the Hudson that look like they belong in a display for a storefront window / Beam Me Up Scotty written in graffiti on an abandoned workmen's trailer / dead breaths

heard two girls talking on campus sometimes I swear I look like a bag lady have a good Christmas you too bye

A Mule on Horseback

'Tis a muddle, and that's all.
—Charles Dickens, *Hard Times*

his head caved in so they took him to the hospital

petting a dead monkey at the zoo

a pass so long that by the time he caught the ball it was moldy and deflated and he was old and senile and put the ball on his head like a hat and fell down like a deck of cards

a fence of body hair

two pigeons on a ledge their heads tucked into their bodies

a tree house for his thoughts

sex-changed priests holding rabid otters using the voice of Elvis Presley to impregnate two-year-old girls from ten feet away

the Civil War jumped out of a history book and darted onto the interstate causing a twenty-car pile-up

after the first five seconds you felt like you'd known him for a million years

flowers opening their mail in the sunlight / blind men shopping for sunglasses

call everything art and shrug

three tons of Pilgrim Rock broken or stolen since 1621

getting out of bed nailing thoughts to the walls / that was easy

she was out to lunch and wasn't ever coming back / he was checking out of the hotel of life / more horror stories / leave your name and message at the tone

murder

chickens pecking at a corpse / blank eyes staring back

self-induced invisibility

notebook thrown from a roof like a telephone / a wind-blown newspaper page pinned against a lamppost / bags balled up in the soul / Saint Ego with Percodan in his beer

she complains that I'm always hiding my words

why bother written at the bottom of the page / a fragment of a fragment / a ghost at the chain saw murderer's house / empty reflection in the mirror each morning

a mule on horseback

a transparent rainbow

perspiring teeth / melted radiator / a wooden clam with a cowboy hat filled with lard / toothpick ventriloquist with a lasso around his neck fleeing from the house / a fish with a lead soda bottle / a two-headed mile made of plastic

their pet ghost standing in the corner no longer lets the children touch it

out of his mind / we'll be right back after these messages

you been on the block for a thousand years and they busted you for that / never got around to it

a gray no-money morning

he psychically willed the authorities to keep the fuck away from him / something is very wrong / quarter-eating pay phones / déjà vu streets of childhood memories / don't despair induce vomiting immediately

half-eaten realities come true / it's all too much take everything away

an early retirement keep dreaming darling

row row row your boat

he was a personalized missing link

a dog in the bar orders a shot of whiskey by barking three times / selling death and dismemberment insurance over the phone

lost borrowed stolen

sticks and stones for entertainment / three wheels and two kilos / the information booth is closed because they have run out of it / cotton candy harps / bruised dreams

he subscribed to the *Daily Abomination* he was well informed

some people just look at you once and automatically hate you

a monkey in a blue leather jacket slithering into Eden and ruining it / a flower in a pink miniskirt / the kitten digging a little grave with a little shovel

competing with the usual strangers at the Nowhere Ball / burning down the house like a cult figure

half-digested light / one-float parades melting like film / blood-stained walls / white sand on the floor

having a hard time believing any of this is remotely real

a rifle made of dirt

plastic chicken eating rubber mice under the stove

another day shot through the head no revelations no signs
no enlightenment

don't wave save it / bad everything / white light ripping him
apart like a paper kite sombrero made of hate / he can't handle
it and neither can she so they got married and faked it / he
stopped signing his name to things

a computer virus deodorant

who sent you

trees cutting down trees / paragraphs digesting sentences of
invisible ink

attack the idols of your enemy

bad-ass kids standing outside the McDonalds on West 4th
Street like dangerous toys / a little boy petting rocks calling
them nice and pretty / down to four cents by the afternoon

smiling at gunpoint in a borrowed castle

petting your cat for you since you are never around

break it down to yes/no questions to save time

she overdosed at the circus

king cripple unholy fool evil twin of Satan's long-lost retarded brother snake-handling idiot savant from Dog Sperm Mississippi self-loathing Prince of Nowhere unready unwilling and unable to face anything mind caved-in like a deflated bag of dirt / ignore all the signs around you / beware of the family

glass eyes in the corpse / a hole in a sock

cryptic hate mail / mental notes / visions of the non-Promised Land worth twenty-seven cents

putting his least foot backward / he set his head on fire and called the police but they wouldn't come

ignore it / pay close attention

scarecrow limbs moving with string head turning on discs heartbeat sustained with electric shocks

lies lies lies love

the tree in the yard fell over so the kids had nothing to swing from

just met you and already don't like you / never change / please change soon a stranger in bed / if he died today he wouldn't have any clothes for his funeral / spray-painted purple ants / reaching for a sound bite under the sofa / losing the way like two blind pallbearers at a flea market

a TV mom taking pills in secret / a neon house plant / a tree coughing foam / talk show audiences breathing life into each other like plastic puppets / if we all care so much then how did it come to this

children should not be raised by anyone

evaporated words running out the door

fourteen-year-old men paying the rent

demented halos in an elephant graveyard

time to turn somebody in

falling down hitting his head on a hidden boulder slipping into Nixon's coma / a green dog on a black lawn / a closed third eye / a black-tie affair / go on ahead without me

smoking a broken flag

blah blah blah ad infinitum

some fucking nerve made into a god by the natives / he aspired to do very little / getting things done in his own weird way

cryptic messages

a midget corpse at the wedding

this is and isn't an artificial heart

letting the train of thought go right by his stop again

he ate the globe in the corner she ate the clock

you've got it all wrong but we'll let it slide for this lifetime but be forewarned

faith-healing a sick flamingo / dead rose in the mail / ringing in the New Year a few months early

the couch was out to get him / his settlement money came in installments like a piecemeal tattoo

thinking about not thinking / sign here on the dotted line / someone put beer in his beer trying to get him drunk

date-raped by a large corporation

Siamese twins slow-dancing in a brush fire

he was a Hebrew prophet for about a week but didn't like it

beware those who underline things in books

mules wearing liederhosen / it really was all an illusion / a
paper bag made of felt at the bar

blessed by Saint Nowhere

the room murdering his posture

a flag nailed to a highchair

don't let the stove go out or the stove will go out

apple butane punch on the leopard skin mantel / rubber house
plants / angry red mailboxes / sour note in the wall / empty
doghouse by the barn

spring cleaning in the fall

when in Rome do as the Swedish do

I was a teenage teenager

decay is king

it was a crude hoax / he dyed his face gold and stood in the shadows like a lawn ornament / catering to complete incompetence and absurd misunderstandings

some people really know how to stare at a wall

never quite the right time for anything / can't can't can't can you won't won't won't will you / picking up pennies from the floor of a dead man on Christmas / a paper car going off a paper cliff

remember to remember

chocolate potato chips

he could never cut a straight slice of bread / she drinks whiskey through a straw made of her own bone which frightens her kids

a cowboy made of rubber glass / the third U.S. soldier has committed suicide in Haiti / a one-eyed shaman laughing at TV commercials / pollywogs attacking the children / feeding the fish other fish

if you are sick do not seek treatment / black magic eating soap / a bird crippled by a kite

give the gift of pain for the holidays

they chiseled teeth for an ugly statue and then it bit them

moving the hand about the paper at will / telephone glued to
the ceiling

she karate chopped the house down

glass hands plastic feet a rubber skull a Styrofoam upper torso

a green towel tried to kill his sister so he had it dyed black

purple flesh clinging to a treasure chest / an alarm clock with
a bad French accent awoke him every morning / the desk bit
into his leg while he was writing a letter to his mother / three
hours passed in two minutes

let others deal with it

grass hair in the sink / water boiling underground

his doctor told him to stay up all night and die / Cain and
Unable came over to visit but got in a fight and had to leave
/ proposing marriage to a painting / invited over for a drink
every two minutes she had no style no class or charm that's
why he married her

houses lighting themselves on fire to break up the monotony

here we go kids hold on

hoping to spontaneously combust

the limits are limited / what will happen next is a mystery /
better luck next life

green water tower looking over its shoulder at paranoid cars /
scorned and shunned like a leper making people nervous
writing in a notebook / killing butterflies in midair with a
single glance / roll over play dead / no-sided coins flipped in
the rain / the downtrodden and dull moving to Never Never
Land / reliving someone else's childhood because his sucked

media darling on a magazine cover / smoking the last ciga-
rette twice / unrehearsed screams

he entered through the exit broke a mirror on a black cat
while holding an umbrella open in the house

a glass tree falls from your hands and shatters on the side-
walk / avoid spontaneity at all costs

building a tower to bolster the other side of his brain

a cricket stopped chirping just as I walked past it must not
have wanted me to hear what it was saying / a boy running
down the beach with a gasoline kite wavering in the wind /
he came in sixty-eighth in a race of just under forty people

a photograph of a photograph / sewing fingernails to a watch band / a three-dimensional belt buckle with a javelin mounted on it / a glacier of Jell-O / using a flamethrower to light her half-mile-long cigarettes / a merry-go-round with electric chairs instead of horses / a peacock with a fresco painting on its tail feathers / a novelty telephone book with wrong numbers / a vitamin contaminated with specks of paint and glass

sitting still for the sales pitch that ended civilization / a stack of counterfeit hundred dollar bills / cavemen sitting around playing Monopoly on a checkerboard

Tom Sawyer

dead soul / batteries not included

insects kicking cans on the way home from school

throwing darts at a life-size target of himself / marching to a drum made of fish

a ballet dancer with a three-foot waistline was last seen leading a pack of wild dogs into the woods / a nun in priest vestments / a camp made in the shadow of a crowbar / a rubber labyrinth

inhaling Silly Putty to see if there were any comic strips in his lungs hosing soap suds off a hearse / tying her shoes before her feet were in them was one of her strong points

visiting his twin sister in Bee Caves Texas / sweating bullets into the chamber of a gun he intended to use / translating a conversation for a turnip and some masonry stone / falling headlong into a well of digested peaches / fishing in a wig with a hat for bait / working nights on the day shift / underestimated by some overestimated by others

a horse in a yellow rain jacket replete with a hood

badly beaten by invisible things

he was the death of the party and everyone loved him / sick and tired but not necessarily in that order

picking his teeth with a lasso / gas pump in hand he looked over at the woman pumping gas beside him and said excuse me miss do you know where the nearest gas station is

practicing voodoo on stained clothing / never seen or heard from again

black lunch boxes filled with pink ice / a tunnel straight to the heart of the question / a tailless fish with cement gills / a spider web catching dew at sunrise long after the spider has moved elsewhere to string its flimsy hammock the owl hooted once and then turned into a graph of coordinate functions / a buck-toothed swan

her life was rated PG-13

the cure for cancer rounding the corner before anyone recognized it

magic wand with no handle

preschoolers in the cigar shop

a candlestick with a frozen hot dog stuffed in it / a harp strung with overcooked spaghetti / a Santa Claus suit made of straw

drinking tea from a wheelbarrow

charcoal-colored frost

he was dead but you wouldn't know it

writing this on a paper bag that blew to my side while sitting on a bench on the Promenade seeing the Statue of Liberty pigeons walking in puddles of melting snow in my shadow behind the bench tugboats crawl the river leaving little books with rippling pages in their wake

the mirror was so small that she never really knew what she

looked like / he was a walking talking idiot

the little boy is afraid of the Michael Jackson doll wants it to
go in the garbage afraid to go into the kitchen until the doll
is hidden from his sight

thoughts scared off like deer

it's now and never

houses laughing like tombs like wind in a grave

having nothing to do all day / feeding the chickens flat tires /
dreams canceled by a power outage

a woman on the subway silver sunglasses at midnight black
earmuffs pink lipstick slip showing at the shins of her parted
black skirt

a popcorn sponge soaking up lime juice / a skydive onto a
thumbtack

coins glued to the sidewalk / empty suitcases / dusty chess-
boards / a one-stringed violin / a ceramic scarf

they raised the fishing nets filled with the day's catch of rot-
ten potatoes

an owl wearing bull horns in broad daylight

violators will be prostituted

a mile of garden hose in a nutshell / the view from the top of your favorite mountain compacted into the void on the top of a mole's head where eyes should be

watching a bullfight in the cheap seats in the sun wishing he was the bull

a seagull swooped down on a pile of seaweed a waitress carried over a bluefish head on a tray and placed it in front of him

canned laughter for a burglar alarm

dead presidents on money did all his talking for him

while recovering from her last recovery she had dreams of Peter murdering Jesus

most of the stars are fake

nuclear bamboo shoots / a blue jay perched on the spine of a phantom / flammable holy water / a rubber band around the atmosphere

breaking the mirror of silence

a ghost ship spotted on the baseball field

the neighbors' missiles made them nervous why didn't they point them at someone else they had been keeping the dog off their lawn it wasn't fair

insects without winter clothing will be dead any day now

yesterday fell down the stairs and tomorrow sprained its ankle playing basketball so who knows when I'll see you next

thirteen prehistoric Animal Crackers

the smell of cow shit in the air like a ghost that hasn't bathed in hundreds of years

piles of firewood cars on blocks in the yard / barns corn silos standing out like giants / nature turned terrorist / flowers crushed under snow

horses that use glue

the faces of famous athletes appeared in the X-rays / home movies of the kids waking up with nightmares

a cemetery small enough to fit in the trunk of a car / insects with snowplows crudely affixed to them lurking outside the mortuary memory like explosives in a feather pillow

he called the mortician himself I'm fixing to die tonight so I'll be right over save you some trouble

listening to the Bible being written in the room next door through cheap walls

caves without plumbing / raft made of light bulbs / drift-wood colliding with a refrigerator / Tarzan steals Jane every Sunday morning on TV

he fell in love with a school of fish and anchored his boat to be with them like books reading each other

spider webs on a cactus / full moon raking the lawn

a couple bucks of gas a Snapple and a candy bar totaled $6.66 oh no he said I check my head every morning in a mirror for the mark he said to the man reluctantly taking his money from behind the counter without saying a word

here is an invisible laundry list submitted as art / no wonder what do they expect / enter it into the record

one too many punches to the head

the TV game show host says if you can't lie to your friends who can you lie to stumbling blindly through the phantasmic halls of academia / white skin purple track marks

one-hundred-year-old paper / an old note taped to the door

a killer confessing over the telephone

handed a note at the bar she unfolded it and read just looking at you makes me want to crawl in my grave a little early she crumpled the note awkwardly threw it at him and tossed her drink in his face

weeks into months of blank diary pages years of empty daily planners / sloppy drunk at the AA meeting / crossed off the birthday card list for good

call work written in blood on the wall beside the memo pad

doctor says the same shit each visit lose twenty-five pounds and get in rehab

wearing a sombrero the size of the room / beer cans in the driveway thrown by forty-five-year-old children

missing the boat but not the passengers / names crossed off old lists

she hired a psychic hitman to ruin his every waking moment / playing the villain in a series of greeting cards

cancel all engagements take all calls tell them to fuck off
that no one gives a shit any longer tell them you won't be in
who needs it

July shot through the head August was murdered in its sleep

robbing graves for gold fillings and skulls which they could
get three hundred dollars a piece for

taking a sip of beer while staring at Antarctica on a map on
the wall he reached over flicked his lighter and held it to a
frayed edge which went up instantly and had to be quickly
put out with a blanket as it spread up the wall in a flash

this is not a dream this is not real / ever meet yourself did it
frighten you

milking a dead cow with invisible fingers

the sun shining all night in midnight bathtubs

it took her thirty-five minutes to become her own self-fulfill-
ing prophecy

sitting on the subway a woman stepped in the car said will
you do me a favor I gave her a look that said I seriously doubt
it I don't speak English what do you want she waved her
hand at me and said forget it stepped back off the train be-
fore the doors closed

impatient people on subway platforms with magnets in their pockets luring trains / pointing at the fire with sticks trying to draw it closer

watching Sinatra footage from a 1986 performance from Sun City she said it's a shame he's lost his lower range he said it's a shame he's playing Sun City she looked back at him as if she couldn't understand what he meant

clay embryo days hatched shattered crossed off the calendar / wind breaking and entering through a keyhole / fruit freefalling from an elevation of fifteen hundred feet / singing the apocalypse to sleep / banal breakthrough after banal break-through

a bird with closets for wings coat hangers and old magazines soaring overhead like packages to the sun

his hearing had gotten so bad that he resorted to saying you can spell that again / these feeble words stranded on paper lifeless inert one-dimensional or less

a moody pasture with no grass for the cows to eat that have to order out for pizza and Chinese food

why persist / bringing us back / the trees looking malnour-ished starved of birds and foliage

hundreds of missing lines / horrible months torn from old

diaries

a lost cardboard Count Chocula mask from the back of a
cereal box

he melted her out of his mind / photographs taken by dead
people with cameras without film / black out-of-tune notes
playing a death dirge on a violin strung with barbwire

she told me that one day the Statue of Liberty would walk
on the water and set the people free and that I was going to
be a singer

under our dead talk down by the sea on my deathbed with
my baby is where I'll be

all too often she found herself wondering what he was doing
when she no longer wanted to think of him at all

cement in a pair of old boots

at a loss for a reason / surrounded by danger and uncertainty
/ hallucinating that the bed got longer at night

most of it has gotten away / walking over thoughts in his
mind / a puddle on the roof of the building below without
sense to come in from the rain

tin cans tied to newlyweds

woken up when he wasn't asleep / a sedated slug after receiving enough shock treatments to stun a herd of cattle / he was afraid of people who believed in things

thinking about nothing in particular / hoping it would just come in a dream / staring at the floor for a living

a plastic World War II helmet with a pipe filled with wheat germ barking out commands and fighting an invisible war

a dead dog / black and white photograph of a mask on a fall sidewalk / frightened always feeling like he was being watched even when alone as a little boy / touching a dolphin in a pool somewhere in Massachusetts surprised that it felt like smooth rubber glass at one point in the show the dolphins wore tiny red fire helmets and put out fires

lucky coin removed from the fourth stomach of an ox

let's not have a president this year

boats docked on asphalt beside the river like chickens that smoke fat cigars

destroying memories by chronicling them

music blaring out of trailer windows / seeing bloody footprints in the snow in the yard one morning data for books that would never be written / a color photo of headless legless armless bodies piled on top of one another painted fluorescent orange / a canopied bed in the dream with a velvet blanket / finding money in a drawer

Dennis Lucas was born in 1968 and received a B.A. in English from Brooklyn College. His musical entity Closed Third Eye rears its ugly head from time to time. He currently resides in West Saugerties, New York.